The First Writing Book

An English Translation & Facsimile text
of Arrighi's OPERINA, the first manual
of the Chancery hand,
with Introduction and Notes by
John Howard Benson.

New Haven and London
Yale University Press

Ninth printing, 1974.

Printed in the United States of America
by The Colonial Press, Inc., Clinton, Mass.

Published in Great Britain, Europe, and Africa
by Yale University Press, Ltd., London.
Distributed in Latin America
by Kaiman & Polon, Inc., New York City; in
Australasia and Southeast Asia by John Wiley
& Sons Australasia Pty. Ltd., Sydney; in India
by UBS Publishers' Distributors Pvt., Ltd.,
Delhi; in Japan by John Weatherhill, Inc., Tokyo.

Library of Congress catalogue card number: 54-11610.

ISBN: 0-300-00301-3 (cloth),
       0-300-00020-0 (paper)

In Memoriam

HENRY EUGENE COE
1894 – 1954
Yale 1917

ACKNOWLEDGEMENTS

Having lived with the problems of this book for over two years, I have not hesitated to inflict them on many friends. Grateful acknowledgement is due for their patient help.

The Rev. Henry K. Pierce and Mr. Erich A. O'D. Taylor were my associates in an earlier venture; I am indebted to the former for starting me on this project, and to the latter for checking the English text when it was completed.

With Mr. Vincent Esposito I discussed many aspects of the Italian, and Miss Susan B. Franklin helped with the Latin texts. Mr. William K. Wimsatt suggested valuable changes in the Introduction and Notes.

At the John Stevens Shop I shared the intriguing complexities involved in the layout of the English pages with my partners Miss A. de Bethune and Miss Nancy Price, as well as with Mrs. Francis Brady and Miss Edith B. Price. Without the coöperation of the latter it would have been impossible to solve many difficult problems.

J.H.B.

FOREWORD

Ludovico degli Arrighi, called Vicentino, who seems to have died in Rome about 1527, is not a forgotten artist. His 'Operina' is well known to contemporary students of calligraphy, to designers, and even to laymen interested in lettering. It is so basic that it is usually given first place in any account of the sixteenth century Italian writing masters. Then why has no one before translated the 'Operina' with explanatory notes, so that we can use the precepts of this acknowledged master in their unadulterated form?

One is tempted to sigh and reflect on the incorrigible negligence of mankind. But there is a better reason in the present case. The task demands scholarly and technical knowledge as well as an eye to practical application. An unusual combination of talents must be assembled, which is not easy to find. John Howard Benson, by rare chance, has all three. With driving enthusiasm he not only mastered the intricacies of Arrighi's early Italian technical expression, but rewrote, time and again,

every line of the text till it closely resembles, page
for page, the original here printed with it.
It is not John Benson's first book on calligraphy.
In 1940, with A. Graham Carey, he published
'The Elements of Lettering', which remains one of
the foremost works on this subject. He has taken
notes for years on early New England tombstones
for a book which should be, if he finds time to write
it, the definitive work on what is our earliest Colonial sculpture. As a sculptor and letterer of
every kind of inscription and memorial, he has
his widest reputation.
This book should find a place not only on the shelves
of scholars and lettering experts, but in schools, and
in the hands of everyone who recognizes the need of
reform in our current handwriting – so formless, so
untutored, so debased by neglect, the typewriter, and
our hectic pace of life.

+

Philip Hofer
Cambridge, Massachusetts
28 August, 1953

INTRODUCTION

The aim of this book is to help those who wish to reform their handwriting. Most of us are dissatisfied with the way we write. This is true whether we were taught to use the pointed pen of the copy-books or the broad stub of 'manuscript writing'. If our instruction stemmed from the copper-plate tradition, we probably write rapidly, perhaps legibly, but almost surely with no delight in the perfection of the writing itself. If, on the other hand, we were taught to make formal disconnected letters slowly with a wide-edged pen, we may have some understanding of the character of good pen strokes, but it is doubtful if we have acquired a running hand rapid enough to meet even the limited demands made on our penmanship today.

Typewriting and other modern techniques have freed us from a heavy load of writing by hand and hence from a need for great speed in writing, but most of us still need to use a pen, and if we wish to use it well we should have models for a hand sufficiently cursive to be practical and with enough character of the edged pen to be pleasant to write and easy to read. Such models for handwriting are found in the 15th and 16th century Italian hands. The best of these for our purpose is the Chancery Cursive: called CHANCERY because used in the Chancery office of the church and CURSIVE because written more rapidly than the Gothic hand used for formal documents. Epistles in the Chancery script were said to be written 'brevi manu' (with a short hand) and were therefore called BRIEFS.

Italian writing books of the first half of the 16th century, notably those of Arrighi, Tagliente, and Palatino, supply us with printed examples of the Chancery letter. Of these the 1522 OPERINA, or LITTLE WORK, of ARRIGHI - otherwise known as Ludovicus de Henricis, surnamed Vicentino - is considered by many today to be the finest of all writing books as well as the first. It has been reproduced in facsimile, without translation, together with Arrighi's second book, in an edition of 300 copies, privately printed in 1926. That edition has an excellent introduction by Stanley Morison, whose scholarly work, together with that of James Wardrop, makes it unnecessary for me to attempt any historical treatment of Arrighi in this book. It is enough to know that he was a master scribe, a type designer of distinction, and that his manual should be familiar to those of us who are interested in good handwriting. The OPERINA is here freely translated and written in a hand based on the original. Its 32 woodcut pages are also reproduced by photo-offset from a copy of the first edition in my possession. I have added notes which deal briefly with the subject matter in its relation to handwriting practice of our day and include some forms revised in accordance with this practice.

Arrighi's own Foreword makes it clear that he had posterity in mind as well as the readers of his own time. If we are to make the most of his examples we must learn some technical facts that to him were obvious, and know something of what has happened since 1522. Before the invention of printing, books were written slowly by hand with a wide pen. The chisel edge of the reed or quill pens used for such formal writing produced a variation in width of stroke dependent on the direction in which the pen moved. For Chancery writing the pen is normally cut square across on the end and is held with its edge at a constant 45° angle to the line on which one writes. It then makes a thin stroke if moved diagonally upwards, thus /, and a thick stroke the full width of the nib if moved diagonally downwards, thus \. If moved in a curve, such an edged pen makes a stroke which varies in width, thus O ∿ (∾ .

These thicks and thins must not be confused with the variations in width produced by pressure on a flexible pointed pen and printed from engraved copper-plates in many 17th and 18th century writing books, thus *AbCdE*. Such letters, although quite suited to the technique of metal engraving, are not the best pen forms. The pointed pen is largely responsible for the sorry state of handwriting today.

In recent years an attempt has been made to teach children to write with a wide pen, forming capitals and small letters carefully without any connecting strokes, thus Print-Script. This 'manuscript writing' reintroduced the edged pen and the formal character of the 15th century book= hands. The method and models, however did not supply the key to the necessary transition into a practical, rapid, cursive hand. At the same time a revival of calligraphy by Edward Johnston and his followers, especially Alfred Fairbank, has restored the Chancery Cursive to its proper place as the exemplar hand for fine writing. In it the strokes of the edged pen are adapted not only to legibility but also to speed.

In order to write Chancery letters we must first procure a suitable pen. Cut properly, a quill is the best of all writing tools because its firm but soft material enables even a sharp edge to move easily across a sheet of paper. But quills are hard to find and difficult to sharpen. In a metal pen the corners of the nib must be rounded enough to move freely without catching the paper but not so much as to lose the thicks and thins. Steel nibs are cheap and many varieties can be tried until one that satisfies is found. Fountain pens are convenient, though most of them have a bump on the under side which must be partially removed, since the under surface of a nib should be flat. Two fountain pens were used for writing this book. One was an English pen, a Swan 'Calligraph' with a medium nib. The other, used for the larger writing, was an Esterbrook with a 'Broad Relief' nib ground for Chancery writing. Both of these pens are cut square on the end and are flat on the under side. Whatever pen we use, it should make its thickest and its thinnest strokes at a 45° angle to the writing line when held naturally between the thumb and first fingers of the right hand. Experiment with pens, inks and papers until you find a good combination of tools and materials.

You should sit upright, with both feet on the floor, and at a desk of suitable height. If the surface of the desk is rough or too hard, a sheet of blotting paper placed under the writing paper will act as a cushion. If the lower part of the writing paper tends to become soiled or greasy, it may be covered with an extra sheet of paper. The light should be good and come from the left side, except for left-handed writers.

Right-handed persons should place the paper nearly square with the desk. Left-handed persons should give the paper a left cant; they

should also use pens with a left skew. The cut
of the pen, the way it is held, and the position
of the paper combine to determine the slant of
the pen's edge and hence that of the thin strokes.

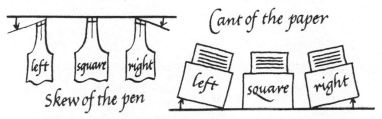

Cant of the paper

Skew of the pen

    Having obtained a good pen and materials,
you should read the English translation of Arrighi
and study his own Italian pages, referring to the
notes for each page. In writing the translation I
have made an attempt to retain the appearance of
the original, though to achieve this completely
was impossible. I ask you to overlook the short=
comings of the English pages. It is Arrighi's
hand that you should study and imitate.

LA OPERI
NA

of Ludouico Vicentino, for

learning to

write

The

Chancery

let-

ter

The Method & Rule for writing the cursive or Chancery letter newly composed by Ludovico Vicentino

Writer of apostolic briefs in Rome the Year of our salvation

· MDXXII ·

⁓: To the kind Reader :⁓

Besought, indeed compelled by many friends,
most gracious Reader, that having regard
for public use & profit not only in this age,
but also for posterity, I would give some ex=
amples of the writing & regular formation
of the characters and particulars of the
letters (which today are called Chancery)
willingly I have undertaken this task: &
since it was impossible to offer enough ex=
amples of my own hand to satisfy all, I have
set myself to study this new invention of
letters and to put them into print, & they
are as close to handwriting as my ability
can achieve. If they do not exactly answer
in every respect, I beg you to excuse me,
since the press cannot entirely represent
the living hand. I hope nonetheless that
by following my instruction you will ob=
tain your desire. Long life, & Health :⁓

Anyone who wishes to learn to write
the cursive or Chancery letter ought
to observe the following forms
&
First he should learn to make these
two strokes, to wit
with one of which begin all
the
Chancery letters.
Of
these two strokes the one is flat and
thick,
the other is slanting
&
thin as you can see here noted

Do
first the
flat & thick stroke
that is - - - with which, reversed
& turning upon itself, one com=
mences;
thus one begins the following letters
- a b c d f g h k l o g s ſ x
x y z
The rest of the Alphabet begins with
the
second stroke, slanting
& thin, ascending with the edge of
the pen and
then
Returning downwards in this way
ı e e' i m n p r t u ij

From the first stroke thick & flat
make this body o ͦ ͘ o from
which then come five letters
a d c g g
The bodies of these letters, which
touch the line upon
which you will
write
must each
be
formed
in
an oblong parallelogram
&
not a perfect square, in this way
namely ▯ ⸫ ⸴ ⸴ ⸴ a ⸴ c ⸴ d g ⸬ g ▯
a d c g g

Understand
then that not only the above
five letters a c d g g
but almost all the other letters are
formed in this :: oblong parallelogram
and not in a perfect
square ◻
because to my eye the cursive
or Chancery letter ought to
partake of the
long
& not of the round : which roundneß
would come if made
from a perfect
square
& not an oblong parallelogram

Perselvering with the Alphabet you will
learn to make this line ſ, beginning it
with the firſt thick and flat ſtroke
⁻ſ⁻ſ
from which the following letters
are derived
b d ff f h k l ſ ſſ ſſ l b ll lb ſl
& that they may be done properly you
will make at the top the
head ſtroke a little thicker than the line.
That thickening is easily
made if you
ſtart the head ſtroke by commenc=
ing it in reverſe, & then
returning backwards
over the same
⁻ſb d f ff h k l l l l l l b b ſ ſſ l l ⁻

Once having learned to
make
the letters
written above, which all com=
mence with the first Stroke thick et
flat as I have said, you will
come to those
that
begin with the second Stroke slant=
ing and thin, as, following along
in this little Trea=
tise of mine
you will by yourself be
able
easily to
Comprehend.

Letters beginning with the second, or
slanting & thin stroke
are the following, Namely
aiee'ij mnpr
tu
which all ought to be equal, save'
that the p and the t should be'a
little taller than the bodies of the other
letters
as I demonstrate by
this example
apatntumpnoturpgrstumputinatmpi
& this greater height of the'p - that is
of the line, not the loop - to my eye'
is more pleasing : of the t, it is so made
to be different from c.

Moreover, since we have two kinds
of s ſ, as you see, & as I have taught
  you of the long one', it remains
    to ſpeak of the smaller
         whose lower
      curve you make greater
           than the'
    upper as you see here'
            s s s
Commence with the first thick and
      flat ſtroke as I have'
            shown
& returning it back on itself curve
    it so that you make an

            s

         as intended

Having now come to the letters x y z
we find that of these the x and y
begin almost in the

same way,
thus ᴜ, crossing in the middle of
the first stroke to make the x, which
in front ought to be no higher than

an a
Let a y be made the same as to height,
in this way

xayaxayaxayayaxy

Of
the z teach yourself to make
it with these strokes as here shown

Then having learned the
Alphabet it is necessary to take care
in putting the letters together that all the
ascenders be'equal, thus b d h k l
with the little top leaning
forward rounded and thick like the
beginning of a c l l
Similarly the descenders ought
to be all the same
length
f g p q s x y ſ
& the bodies of all the letters ought
to be even both below and above
in the manner here
shown
A abcdemfmgmhiklmnopgrstustumyxyꝛ

Et because' the' letters of the'
Alphabet are made', some in one
Stroke without lifting
the pen from the paper, some' in
two Strokes
Jt has seemed to me' proper to tell
you which are' those made with
one' e' which with two Strokes.
Those' that are' made
with one'   Stroke'
are the'   following
namely
a b c g h i l l m n o q r s ſ u y z
The reſt of the' Alphabet
is
made' in two Strokes
d e' f k p t x &

So, my Reader, you must know that of
the small letters of the Alphabet,
some may be tied with those that follow,
some may not : Those that may
be tied with their followers are here
written, namely, a c d f i k l m
n ſ s t u
Of which a d i k l m n u are tied
with any that follow : But c f ſs t
tie only with some : The rest of the
Alphabet, to wit, be eg h o p g r x y z
ought not to be tied to the letter
following. But to tie or
not to tie, I leave to
your judgment
provided that
the letters be
equal.

16

See below an example of the letters
that can be joined with any that follow
to Wit
aa ab ac ad ae af ag ah ai ak al am an
ao ap aq ar as af at au ax ay az
The same can be done with d i k l m n u .
The ligatures for c f s ſ t are
written
below
ct , ſa ff fi fm fn fo fr fu fy ,
ſt ſt
ſf ſſ ß ſt , ta te ti tm tn to tg tr tt tu
tx ty
Concerning the other letters of the Alphabet,
which are b e g h o p q r x y z ʒ
one ought not to tie any to
the letter following .

& in order that your writing may have
more facility, you make'
all the
characters, or letters, tilting
forward in this
manner
Thus

Virtue surely outdoes all things :~

Not wishing that they should tilt
too much, I have' made
this example to show the way these
letters
ought to lean
forward .

Notice, gracious Reader, that since
I have said that all of the
characters should be tilted forward,
you must understand this
is for the small letters

A

I would like your Capitals always
to be drawn upright

&

the strokes to be firm &
without any wavering at all,
otherwise, it seems to me
that
they will have
no
Beauty

From line to
line the'
distance of anything you
write' in Chancery
letters ought
not to be too large, or too small, but in
between .
& the distance from word to word equal
to the width of an n: From letter to
letter within the ligature,
leave' as much white as within the legs
of an n .
Maybe' you will find it impossible' to
keep this rule', if so, strive to take counsel
with your eye, and to satisfy it; thus
you will achieve the best
Composition.

Certainly enough has been demonstrated
of my method of writing these
Chancery letters, that is the small ones:
Hence it remains to tell
that which pertains
to the Capitals,
all of which ought to begin with the two
strokes that I have described for the
little letters, the one flat & thick, the oth=
er, slanting & thin
in
this
way

-/-/-/-

Good Capitals are not difficult to make
when with the small letters
you have acquired a
firm hand, &
most of all I should tell
you the two beginning strokes of the
Small are the same as those for the Large:
as you continue to write you
will recognize the
similarity
Nothing else needs to be said save that
you should now learn to Make the
Capitals, as drawn
for your espe=
cial example

A A A B B C C D D E E F F
G G H H I I K K L L M M
M M N N O O P P Q Q
R R S S T T I U U U V
X X X Y Y Z Z & & &cet

~: Ludouicus Vicentin. scribebat :~

✦ Rome anno domini ✦

• MDXXII •

A a b c d e m f n g m h i k l m n o p q r s t u m x m y z •

• u •

~: Examples for training the Hand :~

A -: cc ab cc d ce e'f c g h i k l m n o p q p g

o r s f t u x x y z Et st sf ss ss stu w w

No Glory comes at the start, but at the end.

Thus is born honor. true &

perfect:

Why enter the field of battle, e˜ then flee'?

Ille' Idem Evicetinus Scribebat Rome'.

A ~:· By favor of God, perfect & Immortal :~

A abcdee´fgghiklmnopqrsʃtuxx
xyxyzZE & J

Such is the ʃtate of man: At evening his courʃe´
is run. Tomorrow he is reborn. Only
virtue conquers proud & horrid
Death.

Ludo. Vicetinus Rome´in Parhione´
ʃcribeba

· ANN · MDXXII ·

To God & Virtue´all things are due´.

A B C D E F G H I K L M M
N O P Q R S T V X Y 3 Z

a b c d e e f g g h i k l m n o p q r s f t u x
x y z z & &

Everything in moderation :
certain
are those
Limits beyond which there cannot be
Right

A A B C D E F G H I K L M N O P Q
R S T V X Y Z

The Blessed held a Middle way

A a aBbc Ɗ de Ɛ Ff Ggh Hi Jk kKLl
M m Nn o p I g Qr R ſtu v V x x y z

z Ȝ ſ &c R r

For indeed all will be done fitly if time is rightly
diſpenſed, & if each day we give ſtated
hours to letters, not being
diſtracted by
other business from reading
something daily.

Eodem Ludɔ. Vicentino ſcribete. vii. auguſti.

In alma Vrbe

F. Petrar. die

Seeking, I followed hope, & vain desire:
Now I have before my eyes a clear glass
Wherein I see myself
& my fail=
ures
& at the last, may I prepare myself,
Thinking
of
my brief life in which
This morning I was a boy, & now
I
am old :~

Brief & irreparable is Time

Reject Avarice, that Queen of unspeakable
faults,
whom all crimes serve with a detestable
devotion:
& truly Avari=
ce
strives for money, for which no wise man
yearns: & imbued as if with evil poisons,
she weakens the body and the virile
mind & neither by
riches
nor
by poverty is her greed made less.

A miser is in no way good, but evil:~

Having knowledge of his own char=
acter
is a mark of excellent wisdom in a man,
Not being deceived by any self love and
so think=
ing
himself good though he is not.
Galenus said this & Vicentinus
Wrote it in the

CITY

Powerful indeed is a man to direct his
own actions if
he
really knows him=
self.

A GOLDEN SENTIMENT

Amantmo. A. Beatmo Caro. Carmo Charmo

Dignmo. Exmo. Excf. R. Pn. Famosmo

Gnoso. A Honmo HONmo. Hon. Illmo

ILLmo. HL. ILLmo. ILLsso illmo. Kco.

ILL. Mtas. Magtia. Magco. Nobilmo. O

Rincipi Presmo. QRtmo Reueren

Scrtmo SaNtas Itt Venlus Vra Xmo

YZ

. Lud Vicentin. Scibebat S

Reader, if you find aught
to offend
In this little Treatise' of Vicenti=
no,
Do not be' amazed, Because it is Divi=
ne'
& not human, to be' quite' without
fault .

No one can dwell here without
defect
Could any man stand free from
sin,
He would be like to God
who alone is perfect.

The end of
the
ART
of
writing the Cursive or
Chancery let=
ter
Printed in Rome from the original
of Ludouico Vicentino,

writer

CVM GRATIA & PRIVILEGIO

Laoperi
na
di Ludouico Vicentino, da

imparare di

scriue=

re

littera Can=

cellaresch=

cha

Il Modo

&

Regola de' scriuere' littera corsiua ouer Cancellarescha nouamente' compos to per Ludovico Vicenti=no

Scrittore' de' breui aplici in Roma nel Anno di' nra salute

✝ MDXXII ✝

A

Al benigno Lettore :~

Pregato piu uolte, anzi constretto da molti amici benignissimo Lettore, che riguardo hauendo alla publica utilita e comodo non solamente di questa età, ma delli posteri anchora, volessi dar qualche essempio di scriuere, et regulatamente formare gli caratteri e note delle lre (che Cancellaresche hoggi di chiamano) uoletier pigliai questa fatica: E perche impossibile era de mia mano porger tanti essempi, che sodisfacessino a tutti, mi sono ingegnato di ritrouare questa nuoua inuentione de lre, e metterle in stampa, le quali tanto se auicinano alle scritte a mano, quanto capeua il mio ingegno, E se puntualmente in tutto no te rispondono, supplicoti che mi facci iscusato, Conciosia che la stampa no possa in tutto ripresentarte la viua mano, Spero nondimeno che imitando tu il mio ricordo, da te stesso potrai conseguire il tuo desiderio . Uiui, e Sta Sano :~

A chiunq3 uole' imparare' scriuere' l'ra
corsiua, o sia cancellaresca conuiene'
osseruare' la sottoscritta norma
&

Primieramente' imparerai di fare' que=
sti dui tratti, cioe --
da li quali se' principiano tutte'
le'

littere' cancellare=
sche',

Deli quali dui tratti l'uno e' piano et
grosso,
l'altro e' acuto et sotti
le'

come' qui tu puoi uedere' notato

Dal
primo adunq̃
Tratto piano e͞ grͦs=
so cioe' - - - che' alla riuersa
& tornando per il medesmo se' incom=
mincia,
principiarai tutte' le'infrascritte'littere'
-a b c d f g h k l o g s ſ x
x y z
Lo resto poi delo Alphabeto se'principia
dalo
secundo Tratto acuto
e' sottile' con il taglio dela penna asce=
dendo et poi
allo ingiu
Ritornando in questo modo designato
· ı e e'ı m n p r t u ÿ ·

Farai dal primo tratto grosso & pia=
no questo corpo o ɾ ɾ o dal
quale ne caui poi cinque littere
a d c g g
Dele quali lɾe tutti li corpi che toca=
no la linea, sopra
la quale tu scri
uerai,
se hanno
da
formare
in
vno quadreto oblongo
et
non quadro perfetto, in tal modo
cioe □ ∴ ɾ. o. a o. ∴ d g ∷ g □
a d c g g

Vltra le' retro=
scritte' cinque' littere' a c d g g
ti fo intendere'
che' anchora quasi tutte' le' altre' lre'
se' hanno á formare' in questo :: qua=
dretto oblungo et non quadro per
fetto □
perche' al'occhio mio la littera
corsiua ouero Cancellarescha'
vuole hauere'
del
lungo & non del rotondo : che' rotonda'
ti veneria fatta quá=
do dal quadro
perfetto
& non oblungo la formasti

Per seguire poi l'ordine de l'Alphabeto im=
parerai di fare questa linea ∫ principiá=
dola con lo primo tratto groſſo et piano
¯∫ ¯∫

dala quale ne cauerai le littere in=
fraſcritte

b d ff f h k l ſ ſſ ſf l b ll lb ſl

&l per fare che habbiano la ragione ſua
li farai in cima quella te
ſtolina un poco piu groſſeta che la linea,
la qual groſſeza tu facil=
mente farai

ſe facendo il primo tratto lo comen=
ci alla riuerſa, &l dapoi
ritorni indrieto per
lo medeſmo

¯ſ b d ff f h k l l l l l h b ſ ſſ ſl ¯

Quando haraj impa=
rato
di fare' le'
tre'antescritte', quali tutte' comin=
ciano da quel primo tratto groſſo e
piano chio tho detto, tr'ne' venerai ad quelle'
che'
con il ſecundo tratto acuto et ſotti=
le' ſe' debbono principiare', come'
ſeguendo in que=
ſto mio
Trattatello facilmente' potrai
da te'
ſteſſo
Comprende=
re'

B

Le littere' per tanto, quali dal Secundo trat=
to acuto Et Sottile' se' princi=
piano, Sonno le' infraScritte', Cioe'
a i e e' i j m n p r
t u
le' quali tutte' deueno eSsere' eguali, Saluo
che' il p et il t hanno da eSsere' un
poco piu altette' che' li Corpi dele' altre'
tre

come' quiui con lo exem
pio Ti dimoStro
a p a t m t u m p n o t u r p g r S t u m p u t i n a t m p i
Et queSta piu alteza del p cioe' dela linea
et non dela panza, a l'occhio mio aſ=
sai piu Satiſface: Del t poi, si fa p farlo
differente' da vno, c.

Ma perche' hauemo due' sorte' di s ſ co=
me' uedi, & dela lunga te' ho riſegnato,
Reſta dire de' la piccola, dela qua=
le' farai che'l uoltare'
di ſotto ſia
maggiore' che' quello
di ſopra
si come' qui vedi ſignato
s s s
Jncominzandola pure' con lo primo tra=
e' to groſso e' piano ch'io
ti'diſſi
& ritornando per lo medeſmo idrieto
voltandolo al modo chel ſia vno
s
che ſintenda

A auemo anchora du dire' de lo x y z
de le' quali Tre' lre' lo x et y comincia=
no quasi ad uno modo
medesmo
cioe' ⌐⌐ cosi, tagliando nel mezo de lo
primo tratto per fare' lo x, et che' dinaci
non sia piu largo che' guanto e' alto
vno a,
Lo simile' farai del y guanto a l'alteza,
in tal modo
xayaxayaxayaxy
De'
La z poi ti sforzera di far=
la con questi tratti' che' qui sonno signati

⌐ 7 z 3 z
s z z
8

Te' bisogna poi imparato
l'Alphabeto, per congiungere' le' lre'
insieme' aduertire' che' tutte' le' haste' siano equali, come' sonno b d h k l
con lo suo punteto i cima
pendente' rotundo e grosetto in modo del
principio de uno c l L
Similmente' le' gambe' de sotto
siano pari a una
mesura

ſ g p g ſ x y ſſ
& che li corpi de' tutte' le' littere' ua-
dino equali cosi di sotto come' di sopra
in questo modo qui-
ui signato
A abcdemsngmhiklmmopqrstustumvxyz

Et perche' de' tutte' le' littere' de' lo
Alphabeto, alcune' se' fanno in uno
tracto senza leuare'
la penna desopra la carta, alcune' in
dui tracti
Mi e' parso al proposito dirti, quali
sonno quelle' che' con vno, quali ql=
le' che' con dui tracti se' facciano,
Quelle' che' con vno
tracto   se' fanno,
sonno le'   infrascrit=
te. cioe
a b c g h i l l m n o g r s s u y z
Lo resto poi de' l'Alphabe
to
Se' fa in dui' Tracti
d e e' f k p t x &

Saperai anchora Lettor mio che' dele'
littere' piccole' delo Alphabeto,
alcune' si ponno ligare' con le' sue' seguen=
ti, et, alcune' no: Quelle' che' si
ponno ligare' con le' seguenti, sonno le'
infrascritte, cioe', a c d f i k l m
n ſ s t u
Dele' quali a d i k l m n u ſi ligano
con tutte' le' seguenti: Ma c f ſ s t li=
gano ſol con alcune': Lo resto poi delo
Alphabeto cioe' b e' e g h o p q r x y z
non ſe' deue' ligar mai con l'ra
seguente'. Ma nel liga=
re', et non ligare' ti
laſcio in arbitrio
tuo, purche' la
littera ſia e=
guale'.

Seguita lo essempio delle lre che pōno
ligarsi con tutte le sue seguenti, in tal mo=
do cioe

aa ab ac ad ae af ag ah ai ak al am an
ao ap aq ar as as at au ax ay az

Il medesmo farai con d i k l m n u.
Le ligature poi de c f s ſ t sonno
le infra=
scritte

ct, fa ff fi fm fn fo fr fu fy,
ſt st

ſf ſſ ß ſt, ta te ti tm tn to tq tr tt tu
tx ty

Con le restanti littere De lo Alphabeto, che
sono, b e g h o p q r x y z ʒ
non si deue ligar mai lra
alcuna seguente

Et accio che' nel scriuer tuo Tu habbi
più facilita, farai che'
tutti li
caraffheri, o uogli dire' littere'
pendano inanzi, ad
questo modo
Cioe'

Virtus omnibus rebus anteit profecto :~

Non uoglio però che' caschino tanto, Ma
cosi feci l'essempio, per
dimostrarti meglio la via doue' ditte'
littere'
hanno da stare'
pendenti.,

C

Nota, gratioso Let tor mio, che' guatunq̃
ti habbia ditto, che' tutti li
caratheri deueno esser pendenti inanzi,
voglio che' tu intendi questo
guanto alle lre' piccole,

Io
voglio che le' tue' Maiuscule' sempre'
siano tirate' drite'
&
con li suoi tratti fermi e'
saldi senza tremoli per dentro, che
altramente', a mio parer
non
haueriano gra
tia
Alcuna

Farai che la
distantia
da linea a linea de cose che
scriuerai in tal littera
Cancellaresca
non sia troppo larga, ne troppo stretta, ma
mediocre
E la distantia da parola à parola sia
quanto e vno n: Da littera ad
littera poi nel ligarle sia
quanto è il biancho tra le due gambe
de lo n
Ma perche seria quasi impossibile serua-
re questa regola, te sforzarai di consigliar-
ti con l'occhio, et à quello satisfare, il
quale ti scusara bonissi
mo Compasso

Credo assai á bastanza hauerti dimostrato
il modo del mio scriuere' littera
Cancellarescha, quanto alle' lré' piccole' :
Hora ci resta da dirti p̃
quanto alle Maiuscu=
le' si pertenga ,
le' quali tutte' se' deueno principiare'
da quelli dui tratti ch'io tho detto de
le' piccole'cioé' l'uno piano et grosso, l'al=
tro acuto, e, sottile'

in

tal

modo

-/-/-/-

Graue fatica non ti fia ad imparar fare le

littere Maiuscule, quando nelle pic=

cole harai firmato bene

la mano, et

eo maxime chio ti ho

ditto che li Dui principij delle

Piccole sonno anchora quelli delle Grandi

come continuando il scriuere, da te

medesimo uenerai

cognoscendo

Non ti diro adunque altro, Saluo che te

sforzi imparar fare le tue Maiuscule

Come qui apresso ri=

trouerai per esse=

pio designato

A A A B B C C D D E C F F
G G H H J J K K L L M M
M M N N O O P P P Q
R R S S T T J V V V
X X X Y Y Z Z & & &cet

~: Ludouicus vicentin. scribebat :~

✦ Rome anno domini ✦

• MDXXII •

A abcdemfmgnihiklmmopqrstumxcmxyz ·
· uf ·

~: Exempli per firmar la Mano :~

A..c o a b c o d i e e f o g h i k l m n o p q p g

o r s s t u x x y z, Et St Sf Sl ß stu w W

No e' Gloria il principio, ma il seguire'. De'
gui nasce' l'honor uero. Et
persetto :
Che' vale' in campo intrare', et poi fuggire'?

Ille' Idem. L. Vicentinus Scribebat Rome'.

~: Deo optimo & Immortali auspice :~

A abcdee'fgghiklmnopqrsstuxx
xyxyzze'& J

Cosi ua il stato human: Chi questa sera finisce'
il corso suo, chi diman nasce'. Sol
virtu doma Morte' horrida
, e, altera.

Ludo. Vice timus Rome' in Parhione'
scribeba.

· ANN · MDXXII ·

Deo, & Virtuti omnia debent,

A B C D E F G H I K L M M
N O P Q R S T V X Y Z Z

a b c d e e f g g h i k l m n o p q r s s t u x
x y z z & &

Est modus in rebus: sunt
certi
demiqs fines
Quos vltra citraqs nequit consistere
Rectum

A A B C D E F G H I K L M N O P Q
R S T V X Y Z

Medium tenuere Beati

D

A a B b c D d e E f f G g h H i j k K l l

M m N n o p l g q r R s t u v V x x y z

z z s q̃ rz ɣ

Fient autem commode omnia, si recte tempora
dispensabitur: Si singulis diebus statutas
horas litteris dabimus, neq̃s
negocio vllo
abstrahamur; quo minus aliquid
quotidie legamus .,

Eodem Lud̄o. Vicentino scribete. vii. augusti.

In alma Vrbe

F . Petrar. die

Segui gia le speranze, el van desio: Hor
ho dinanci agliocchi un chiaro specchio
Dou io veggio me stesso
el fallir
mio.
Et quanto posso al fine m'apparecchio,
Pensando
al
breue viuer mio nel quale
Sta mane era un fanciullo, & hor
son
vecchio :~

Breue & irreparabile Tempus

Reginam illam procacium uitiorz Auaritia
fuge,
cui cuncta crimina detestabili deuotione
famulantur,
Que quidem Auari=
tia
studium pecunie habet, quam nemo sa=
piens concupiuit : & quasi malis ve=
nenis imbuta, corpus animumiqz
virilem effoemi=
nat

neqz copia neqz inopia minuitur

Auarus i nullo bonus i se aut pessimus :~

Hoc excellentis est sapien=
tiæ
hominem sui ipsius habere notitiam,
Nec ex dilectione, quam habet in se=
ipso falla
tur
Et bonum se repute⁊ cum non sit.
Diĉtaba⁊ hoc Galenus: Scribebat
Vicentinus i

VRBE
Potens quippe est homo suos quosqȝ
aĉtus dirige=
re
seipsum si agnoue=
rit.

AVREA SENTENTIA

Amant.mo .A. Beat.mo Car.o .Car.mo .Char.mo

Dign.mo .E.mo. Cxf.sa .R. Pu. Famos.mo

Gnoso. A con Hon.mo. Hon. Ill.mo

Ill.o .Ill. Ill.ma .Ill.880 Ill.mo .Kr.co

Ill. M.tias. Mag.tia Mag.co. Nobil.mo. O

Rincipi Pres.to .R.mo Reueren

Ser.mo San.tias T T Venz. us Vra X.mo

YZ

.ua & Vicentin. Scribebat.

Lettor, se' truoui cosa che'
t'offenda
Jn questo Trattatel del Vicenti=
no,
Non te' marauigliar, Perche' diui=
no
Et non humano, é quel, ch' é senza
menda.

Qui viuer non si puo senza
defetto
Che' chi potesse' s tar senza pec=
cato
Seria simil á Dio
ch'é sol perfetto

*Finisce
la*

ARTE

*di
scriuere littera Corsiua
ouer Cancellares=
cha
Stampata in Roma per inuentione
di Ludouico Vicentino,
scrittore*

CVM GRATIA & PRIVILEGIO

NOTES

The numerals refer to both the Italian & English
pages. These should always be studied together.

2··· cursive ⹀ I have often used the archaic long s, 'ʃ'
in order to keep the original appearance. It need
not be confused with f since ʃ has no crossbar.

3··· e̓ & e̓ ⹀ The ampersand is a monogram
for 'et', the Latin 'and.' I use it in various forms,
& & & , as does Arrighi in the Italian.

3··· preʃſ cannot entirely represent the living hand ⹀
The OPERINA was printed from blocks cut on the
side grain of wood. These are amazing in their ex⹀
actness, but inevitably the thin strokes are wider
than if made with a pen. Photo-offset gives us a good
reproduction of writing, but even if the translation
were written in a hand identical with Arrighi's
own, which it certainly is not, the effect of the pages
would be different from that of the woodcut text.

4 ··· Anyone ≤ 'Chiunque' is literally 'whoever'. In order to keep Arrighi's initials and page arrange= ments, I have used many similar free translations.

4 ··· observe the following forms ≤ Arrighi begins with the sound advice that we look at his examples and study them. This implies learning his let= ter shapes until they become mental patterns; hence I translate 'norma' (standard) as 'forms'.

4 ··· two strokes, to wit ‒/ ≤ As Arrighi says, any small letter begins with one of these. Palatino, in his 1540 writing book, added the upright ı and the thick diagonal ◥. You must understand that the variation in width of these four straight lines, ‒/ı◥, is due to the fact that the pen is not pointed but has an edge of some width and that the edge is always kept at a 45° angle to the line on which you write. The weight ‒ ᴧ a ‒ of the writing is determined by the ratio between the width of the nib and the height of the letter. In the Chancery hand the nib width is about one fifth of the body height of the small letters. It is very im= portant that your capitals are not higher than

34

one and one half times the height of the small
letters or seven and one half pen widths, thus.

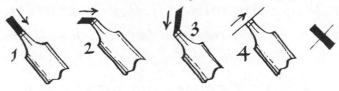

The little black squares are made by holding
the pen horizontal, and represent the full width of
the nib since the pen is cut square across on the end.

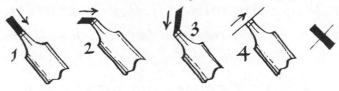

The thick diagonal (1) is also full pen width, but
Arrighi's flat and thick stroke (2) is not; (3) is
not even as wide as (2), and his slanting and thin
stroke (4) made with the pen's edge is a hair line.

5 ··· reversed & turning upon itself ✠ Arrighi here
tells us to begin the letters with the flat and thick
stroke (2), by moving the pen first from left to right
and then back over the same from right to left,
thus ᷓ a. This is not true of the X y z.
In these letters the first stroke moves only from
left to right. Today we begin these letters with the
slanting and thin stroke (4), thus X y y z.

5 ··· b = Arrighi makes b thus ℔, like a closed h.
This stroke sequence has many advantages.

5 ··· h = Today we usually end an h like an n.
Arrighi's h is a very common early form.

5 ··· k = Arrighi's little serif is unnecessary, k.

5 ··· q = This Q is too like a g. q or q is better. In
any writing there should be enough uniform=
ity, or similarity of structure, for letters to go
well together, but also enough diversity so that
each is clearly legible. The h and the q are now
very rarely used because they are not clearly
distinguished from b and g if carelessly written.

5 ··· Returning downwards in this way ⸀1. = It is
natural to begin an upright stroke in the direction
of the pen's edge, thus allowing the ink to start
flowing well from the nib and making at the
same time a delicate beginning to the stroke ⸀1.

5 ··· e = Arrighi's e was made in two strokes, thus
⸀℮². This stroke sequence has the advantage of
being the same as that of the capital ⸀Ɇ³, and its

36

form is also easily kept even when made rapidly.
Teach yourself to make an *l* in this way, *l¹⁴ l²*.
If you cannot, at least be careful that your looped
l is made thus, *l*, not thus, *l*.

6 ··· this body *ᴏ⁻ᴦᴏ* ⧺ This is the basic construction
of the Chancery letter, as Arrighi rightly implies.
You must practise the five letters *a c d g q* and
learn to make the body *;; ⁻ᴦᴏ a* with accuracy
and ease. By making this pattern *aaaaa* you
will find that its dominant movement is that
of an underhand wavy- *ᴜᴜᴜᴜᴜᴜ* -line. This
is a rhythm which *i l o t* and especially *u*
also share. You must never allow it to degen=
erate into an angular ZigZag- *ᴠᴠᴠᴠᴠᴠ* - line.

7 ··· almost all the other letters are formed in this
oblong parallelogram ⧺ If we develop Arrighi's
construction, *⁻ᴦᴏ a*, into a pattern of
two parallel lines and an ellipse with
an axis of greater slope between them,
from this diagram you can derive the main
strokes of many letters, as follows:

37

$\mathcal{H}$ a b c d h i l n o p q r u

Other letters are also related to the parallelogram.

k e j k p g. f g t o o s

y v w y y z m m

The uprights are often closer in M than in n.

7 ··· partake of the long and not of the round ≠
You should strive to maintain the long form
and not allow speed to spread the letter shapes.

8 ···returning backwards over the same ī ≠ In rapid
writing some make the headstroke from right to left
only, thus ī, or omit it entirely if the upright is
made without lifting the pen, thus all. You may
use the slanting and thin stroke to begin the
upright, thus ʾl. Avoid loops - loops- as such
unnecessary parts always make for illegibility.

(g) ··· haraj ·· venerai ≠ On this page in these Italian

words there are j and v, not common in 1522.

10 ··· m n p r ≈ When we practise these letters we find that their underlying pattern is that of an overhand arched- mmmm- line. bh and k also belong in this group. One must practise to be able to change from the overhand to the un= derhand movement and vice versa with ease, not allowing either pattern to become zigzag.

minimum not uuiuimuun
In good writing there should be a balance of the waved and arched rhythms. The use of the looped ℓ and underhand b makes this more difficult to maintain since the waved rhythm tends to predominate. Arrighi often instinctively inserts m s in a compact line of letters, as on this page, partly to maintain such a balance.

10 ··· equal ≈ Here Arrighi refers mainly to the fact that the bodies of small letters should be equal in height. Letters will also be equal if they are similarly constructed in the parallelogram.

10 ··· to my eye is more pleasing= A great virtue in

Arrighi's instruction is that he is not afraid to be guided by his sensitive eye rather than by rules.

10 ··· of the t ≋ It is important always to have the crossbar of the t level with the top of the body, thus at - (not higher, thus at). Every · t · should be crossed immediately after the upright is made, and the bottom hook should be small.

11 ··· two kinds of s∫ ≋ Today we rarely use the long ∫. Make the small one · s · carefully as shown.

12 ··· x y z ≋ These letters are made up largely of diagonal strokes, and together with v and w introduce a new rhythm - WWW ·. These diagonal letters give variety to the regular structure of the Chancery hand. The more cur= sive form y may replace y, but it is best made thus y - (not thus y) - to be distinct from ij.

12 ··· in front ought to be no higher than an a ≋. Unlike a z which is often made higher, thus az.

13 ··· putting the letters together ≋ Arrighi here refers to the grouping of letters into words, not

to tying them together. He deals with that later.

13 ··· all the same length ≈ Uniformity demands
that ordinarily the ascenders and descenders
be of even height, though sometimes there may be
a reason for inequality, as in the double f, ff.

14 ··· two strokes ≈ Without the headstroke d can
be made in one stroke, as can k without the
serif. & is best made in two strokes, thus {&.

15 ··· some may be tied with those that follow, some
may not ≈ It is best when first writing the chan=
cery hand to learn the simplest forms and to
practise them without tying any of them together.

a b c d e f g h i j k l m n o p q r s t u v
w x y y z & 1 2 3 4 5 6 7 8 9 0

When these forms are thoroughly learned, some
can be tied together, as Arrighi recommends.

15 ··· of which adiklmnu are tied with any≈
These are tied with the slanting and thin stroke

41

moving upwards diagonally from letter to letter.

15 ··· But to tie or not to tie I leave to your judgment.
Here again Arrighi's wisdom is evident. Uniform=
ity and good structure are more important than rules.

16 ··· The same can be done with diklmnu. Today
we also add c and h to these letters which tie
with any other by means of the thin diagonal.
Arrighi's b, the looped e, p and even s are
often now tied in this way, thus budapest.

16 ··· The ligatures for cfsſt. These fall into two
groups; the horizontal and the overhead ligatures.
Arrighi shows the horizontal tied strokes of f and t.
t should be tied at the top only, thus letter,
not closed both above and below, thus letter.
In rapid writing ovw are often tied together
horizontally at the top of a word, thus wove.
If such ties seem heavy, because they are made
with the thick and flat stroke, a short diagonal
thin stroke can be substituted, thus woven.
This is lighter in weight, but a more complicated
movement is involved. r and e are often tied

in this way, thus here. The overhead ligatures
are rarely used today, even though they are both
legible and decorative. ﬀ ﬂ ct st st ſs

16 ··· one ought not to tie any to the letter following≈
Actually Arrighi does occasionally tie some
of these letters, a striking example being the
ho of biancho on page (19), although this
may have been a mistake in cutting the block.

17 ··· &≈ It has been suggested that this form
of ampersand may have a special meaning
such as 'e pero che', i.e. 'and for that reason.'

17 ··· that your writing may have more facility≈
Learning the Chancery hand is a task which
must be undertaken in stages. First the letter
forms should be learned and written slowly, then
they should be written more rapidly. Finally
after much practice the hand acquires kinaes=
thetic, or muscular, awareness, and the letters
flow easily from the pen. Chancery letters could
be written vertical, but tilting them makes writing
easier. As Arrighi says, they should not tilt too much.

18 ··· *Capitals always to be drawn upright* ≋ Chancery
small letters inherited their tilt from the Caroline
minuscule, but vertical capitals are a heritage from
the square capitals of classic Rome. In practice
Arrighi often tilts his capitals, witness his V and
M, and particularly his G, all on this page.

18 ··· *without any wavering at all* ≋ Only by much
practice can you acquire a sure and firm hand.

19 ··· *From line to line the distance* ≋ As ascenders and
descenders are normally equal to the body height
of the letters, it follows that the height of the body
should not exceed one third of the space between the
lines. The ascenders of any letters will
then clear the descenders of the line above.
The rules of spacing as set forth on this page are
invaluable, but even more important is Arrighi's
admonition - that we look at what we are writing,
satisfy our eyes, and thus achieve good spacing.

20 ··· *ought to begin with the two strokes ·· in this way* ≋
Although it is true that each of Arrighi's capitals
will begin with one of the two strokes ⁓ he has

described, it is more important for us to know the
basic letters from which his beautiful flourished
capitals were derived. Below we show the capital
letters at their simplest, except for a slight tilt.

A B C D E F G H I J K L M N
O P Q R S T U V W X Y Z

21 ··· Good capitals are not difficult to make＝ You
should learn a logical stroke sequence for capitals.

Make C G J J L S U V W and Z in one stroke.
B D K M N O P Q R T X Y in two,
and ¹/₂\³ ¹L²⁄₃ ¹²⁄₃ ¹²¹³ in three strokes. Capitals
are best made slowly. With skill B D O and Q
can be made in one stroke, but do not hurry them.

21 ··· drawn for your especial example ＝ After we have
made the simple capitals well, Arrighi's examples
as shown on page (22) give us many variants
with which we can enrich our own writing.

23 ··· Examples for training the hand ＝ In these last
pages we find examples to copy. It has seemed best

45

not to change Arrighi's decorative signatures. On this page we find the only Ws in the Operina. WW

24 ⋯ g ≋ Notice this variant of g in the small alphabet.

25 ⋯ AA-Z ≋ These capitals are difficult to write. Being typographic in character, they can only be made by changing the 45° slant of the pen.

26 ⋯ In alma Vrbe ≋ 'In the fostering city', Arrighi, a native of Vicenza, wrote the Operina in Rome.

27 ⋯ Seeking ≋ This word was added to supply an S. The quotation is from Petrarch's - 'Triumph of Time'.

28 ⋯ Que' ≋ e' stands for ae in 'Quae' and 'pecuniae'.

30 ⋯ Amant^mo - X^mo ≋ Study Arrighi's abbreviations as they are excellent examples of free decorative writing.

31 ⋯ aught to offend ≋ Arrighi, one of the greatest scribes of the Renaissance, in this little poem shows us a humility which adds to his stature.

BIBLIOGRAPHY

The Calligraphic Models of Ludovico degli Arrighi.
Introduction by Stanley Morison = Privately printed.

Arrighi Revived.
James Wardrop =   Signature' No. 12.

A Book of Scripts.
Alfred Fairbank =   Penguin Books.

Writing and Illuminating and Lettering.
Edward Johnston =   Sir Isaac Pitman & Sons.

The Elements of Lettering.
J. H. Benson and A. G. Carey = McGraw-Hill Book Co.

A Handwriting Manual. The Dryad Writing Cards.
Alfred Fairbank =   The Dryad Press, Leicester.